# menu

CU00865162

# Italian salad

this salad's a pleasure to make
peeling cucumbers a cue
to indulge in a quick pick-me-up
caress of cool astringent on skin
refreshes memories as flesh

sliced white into a flat glass dish
joins vine-ripened-red tomatoes
fine curls of purple Spanish onion
sea salt seasoned, sprinkled sugar
wine vinegar slurp and now for oil
always Italian virgin first press

metallic crack of seal breaking
back in time, the kitchen at Hillary Crescent
where Dad opens the bottle, we all jostle
for first nose over the neck

to breathe that little bit
of foreign air

# Funny how the garlic

A rope of garlic;
fine green hairs, autumn planted

have grown to these purple, pungent globes
already paper-bagged.
after years of empty seasons, this is good.

I'd almost forgotten how;
had to plait it backwards
as once I braided my hair
laying a heavy rope
between my shoulder-blades
snaking down my spine
so my breasts parted and pointed
and you would do that
slow thing with your tongue
grazing from peaks to valley
humming deep in your throat, while my fingers
flickered in my hair
so sometimes
the braid was abandoned
and two snakes flew through the night
one coming undone
just before the other

sometimes, at night
I didn't braid, but coiled
my hair high on my head
fixed with a pair of chop-sticks

later, with me riding above you
you would reach up
take out the sticks
and laugh, as my hair
tumbled down over us
like a curtain
to our secret cave

now I wear my hair short
I hadn't thought of you in years
funny how the garlic
brought you back

**child's play**


I've been cooking today
two cakes, Ken and Barbie
Ken lies back holding his erection
with that little boy "look at my lollypop" look
*with this, I can move the world*
Barbie is distinctly disinterested
doesn't even blink
as I snap off Ken's penis
crunch it between my strong, white teeth
and swallow
then I rip the cheating heart
right out of his chest
to use in a packed lunch for Barbie.
I'm sending her to a good school
(Not Bryn Mawr, she hasn't any hair on her legs)
maybe UCLA Santa Cruz
where she'll meet Feral Sheryl
the Trailer Trash Barbie, and after a brief affair
they decide they're better as friends
move to San Francisco
where echoes of the beaten hearts
of Beat Poets still resound
from City Lights
where now you can buy sex toys as well as poems
    -    you want a chocolate vibrator with that?
and go home for a really good wank
while heartless sexless Ken
cleans up my kitchen.

## Don Pesto

spicy mystery of basil's
viridian fragrance
pounded with pine tree's
heart and seeds

marble-crucible-melded with
pungent garlic;
crushed cloves
pulsed rhythmically

golden oil squeezed
from gethsemane's fruit
and a final touch
of acidity

my mouth waters
for you, fresh
saying 'cheese'
and smiling

as you spread
my daily bread
so temptingly

## Eating whitebait in the dark

Overnight Kapiti Island
moved closer,
almost near enough
to reach out and rub
the hills' rough scrub flanks.

I went dawn-wading
in whitebait waves
for this morning feast;
translucent fritters of
essence of fish
pan-fried in butter and egg white -
I eat, ecstatically,
my eyes squeezed shut
because I can't bear
to meet theirs.

# I wrote down your mother's recipe for borscht…

…now the words create her face, eyes fixed on mine
anxious to know I'd understood – her accent
always thick; anger or joy could prompt
a dozen different languages. Worn hands
cupped to show sizes of the handful of rice
the heap of dried red beans. *beef bones*, she stresses
grating beetroot and carrot, cubing potatoes.

When she says 'tomato sauce' she means real tomatoes
vine ripened. *check for sourness.* she peers at me now
unsure of the word. *maybe you need some vinegar.*
*Shredded cabbage last. Fry chopped onions black*
*and crunchy, for on top of the dollop of cream.*

Her mother's kulak voice tumbles down the tunnel
of a hundred years of gulags to me, moving time
through family, passing on unending recipes for love.

## Heaven

driftwood stick
poked into rocks
at low tide on a west coast beach

how to tell you
the salty surge
about my thighs
describe the weight
of catch
the slow careful
withdrawal

triumph; the angry clack
of slick black skitter
in the tin

and later
boiled in seawater
red legs cracked

we extract
the sweet feast

**oooops**

     as she checks
supermarket eggs
        for freshness
       her palm curls
   memory response
         to warm
     secret heft
of newlaid life
  her fingers

slip

**Peach**

this fleshy globe
furry where light falls

could be cheek
breast
or buttock

does it matter?

bite

# Bitter in my mouth

The summer we lived at Ahipara
I wanted to catch my own fish.
At low tide I dug pipis for bait,
tried to fingernail-pinch that
muscle tongue and mostly failed,
dodging angry squirts of salt water.
Then at the headland
I wove a hook through the soft flesh
and cast into the tide now turned
and coming in.
The line went taut;
*Caught in rock* I thought,
heaved to pull it free -
the world paused. Over my head
a red-gold butterfly soared
trailing a kite tail wake of diamonds
„til it landed on rocks and
time began again, the fish
flapped and struggled, wings closed
like folded fans, colours fading
as I watched. Its glow dulled
like a light going out.
I took it home still on the hook.
My father roughed up my hair,
said *Not bad, for your first*
named it *butterfly cod*
showed how to scale and gut it,
my mother cooked.
Its tiny bones
hurt to swallow.
I kept seeing it fly.
Each bite of the life
I'd taken and must eat
took longer, until
my appetite was gone.

## Andre Breton and the case of the missing banana

This city blows big time, since you've flown
to London. Even the economy is depressed.
I had to find a flat-mate, whose financial contributions
allow me to wallow in all-day cartoon shows
pajama-clad and reality-adjusted.

She is strange about the placement
of things, and tweaks in secret.

Today she's arranged the book-case by colour.
Andre Breton is in there
getting acquainted with 'Favourite Recipes'
while I tune in to lose myself in the tube.

There's a mess in the kitchen
when the drone comes home, and asks
about her banana
(she has issues with food).

'Breton took it' I tell her
playing the sleuth
'he wanted to try a new recipe'
and I show her the banana-skin
book-marked at 'Elvis's Favourite
Deep-Fried Peanut Butter
and Banana Sandwich'
as proof.

## From the cupboard

Of course the cupboard clears its throat
as it opens -
Rimbaud taught it.

I take out my breakfast, and note
these bananas grew in Ecuador
these oats, in Canada
this sugar came from Fiji;
all gathered here
to build my body.

How strange, and with what patience
I become United Nations

## The poetry barbecue

The workshop at the dementia unit was well attended.
I read some of my poems, we talked about them

then went on to construct one as a group.
I asked them for words meaning summer

*how does it feel, taste, smell, and look to you?*
wrote them down, played and re-arranged.

Jan said *no more raincoats* Bill *children playing
in the distance* - they all agreed distance was needed

and on strawberries, except Mila who wanted raspberries
but was voted down. Ice-cream, salty skin

lawnmowers, the smell of cut grass. barbecues with
onions frying, sausages burnt crispy. They all like that.

Some cried but couldn't say why. They want me back
next week, we're having a poetry barbecue.

## That's gnocchi

It took ages to find
the right potatoes here – floury
(back there I'd walk outside
and dig them up, best Blyton stock
that mashed like meringue, so light
or grew a golden crust beside the roast)

I prick each tuber twenty times
thinking of my garden
(raking slashed grasses, autumn dried
over the potato bed, layered with ash
compost and soil, all level. After planting
when dark green leaves appear, hilling begins)
dry them, place in a hot oven to bake
until skins crisp. break them open to steam
and while still hot, push their flesh
through a grater

work in flour with ring-freed fingers
(this is the soothing part;
kneading dough, feeling change)
if it's sticky, add more flour
until the warm ball is smooth and shiny.
Cut into portions, always cover
each cut surface with a drift of flour.
Roll one by one, like play dough
making snakes

take a dinner fork, prongs down.
make 1" cuts along the snake
(cover cuts in flour)
press each portion against the tines
with your thumb. leave lines
on one side, a dent on the other.
Place on a floured tray to dry
or freeze immediately

The night Terry arrived
bringing gifts of prawns and oysters
I made a Frida Kahlo sauce and gnocchi.
How easy it was then
with wattle trees dancing
outside the kitchen window.

## A piece of my day

If you could see the impossible beauty
of this half-melted sugar Fibonacci
on my glass tea-cup's side -
this diamond feather lace-web delta -
you'd smile, too.

## Stirring sugar

The cup of black coffee
made rings on the
classified columns
of day old newspapers.

You stared through the window
already somewhere else

while I stirred sugar
into the silence
between us.

## Hunger

We eat Weetbix with sugar and hot water,
Golden Syrup on pikelets and scones,

consume my father's body in overtime each Tuesday
and Thursday, every Saturday morning,

devour my mother's love and spit out bitter,
gnash and gnaw at each other.

Time's tapeworm already brings
peace-keeping wars he has no time for,

new ways to do the only things she knows;
we only know that we want more.

We eat bread and dripping, grin
like pickled peaches

do the dishes, sweep the floor
then run outside and howl.

## Spaghetti sauce

An all day thing, this simmering
spaghetti sauce; attempt to approximate

old perfection from memory and little else.
Ingredients here are slightly different, subtle

changes need constant tastings
while aroma curls like a comfortable cat

through the house, memories of meals
and people forever elsewhere now, exact

conversations gone, leaving feelings for words
as well-loved faces, relaxed, smile again

so sadness is a savoury, an undertone
like garlic, adding depth to flavour

permeating and softening 'til swallowed
with gusto, and a satisfying slurp

## Balancing the creative budget

Drizzle olive oil
in a cast-iron pan,
add chopped onions
then garlic

meat
capsicum
and hot chili
(*breathe in the smoky*
*charred smell*)
sauté.

*juggle budgets*
*subtract from phone bill*
*buy green glass*
*needed for the window*
*still a dream*

When ingredients are browned
crumble-textured, dry
add plum tomatoes, ripe and soft
some salt
a wineglass of red
a fist of pinto beans
and slow simmer

*pour more wine*

*the image solidifies -*
*final design*

just before serving
stir in fresh herbs
corn and green beans
garnish with sour cream

*if I don't talk*

*to anyone*
*for a month*
*I can build the window too.*

# I tell my mother stories to replace the ones she's lost

Let's pretend
we're in Havana
between hurricanes.

You can tell your stories of whales
to the gringo who buys you mojitos
each afternoon in that small bar
on the Malecon;
he'll write them down and become famous
you'll be a housewife in New Zealand.

The revolution is perpetual,
change is always imminent.


Your skin has split
here and there -

your shoulder blades poke through
and on the leading edge
grow feathers.

I wonder, should I feed you
heaps of golden grain
ambrosia
or meat?

## A birthday poem

a broken fan belt, and we
without stockings, for the heat

drew straws for one to walk
to the highway
hitch a ride to town
and bring a new part back

the boy who won
(my cousin's friend, city boy, Australian)
was frightened by cows
coming home to pasture after milking;
he climbed a tree and stayed there

meanwhile we waited
boiling ditch water
in a hubcap, for tea

we shared a chocolate bar

sweet, the green sounding hills
and silent yellow sea




## On Cutting Asparagus

dew-wet
mornings
walking early
to the rows of
purple phalli
thrusting hard
into the pearly
lover, Dawn, before
she speeds by
springing wild and
male and errant
dragon teeth to
harvest daily
pride and arrogance
apparent
cut them off!
I do it gaily
left uncut
becoming thyrsus
favourite of the
wild Maenad
grasped with love
by Dionysus
passion that the
reason forbad
snip! the organ
music falters
Satyrs and Sileni
mourning
one last note of
morning psalters
drifts away
into the morning

**Paneta Street***

The launch of the bread and butter pudding book
took place in a bookshop full of old words
squeezed awkwardly to fit between Dylan music
and an ancient picture of the hairy man.

The press gallery, perched on a plastic chair,
flash-strobed accompaniment to the speech
by someone so famous they needed no introduction
and I still don't know who he was.

The rotund poet was self-effacing -
he presented only voice, beard and long grey hair.
His poems shuffled out shyly, squinted in the
dusty light, dimmed by much spider work

and hid amongst disposable wine cups
on the counter. Jack London called to the wild
from the top of shelves marked 'Women'
while a boy discovered gold, and collected it.

The usual suspects ate egg sandwiches without crusts.
None had curly hair except me, drinking wine
in the shadows with Anais Nin and Marilyn French.
The word canoe sailed without sound. I went home early


* title of a book of poetry by Michael O'Leary




**Yes I knew Richard**

we'd bought mud crabs
had them temporarily
in the bath
nippers tied, safe

(we hosted dinner the next night,
chef wanted them live)

when an eccentric millionaire
politician friend dropped in
to visit

next day we took seafood
to the country, and feasted

the Sunday papers featured

big pictures of Richard

who'd bought every crate
of live mud crabs
at the Fish Markets
driven to the beach
and set them free

*go in peace, my brothers*


## the $18,000 vanishing croc burger

It was raining hard, as if
air had always been liquid,
we're sitting around drinking tinnies
when Tom who once worked
on croc farms pointed out

the Fitzroy was in flood -
soon crocs would swim
over fences, gather
at a certain bend in the river. That started
a hunger for a good croc burger.
Skinned and sliced, croc tails
make perfect patties.
We built and lit the fire —
to cook croc properly
you need a big heap of embers —
grabbed the 308s, jumped into
the 'Cruiser and drove
to the coast, a half hour sober drive
but we took longer, to arrive
where crocs gathered
when the flood went through,
turned on the spotlight
caught eyes
let fly with about 30 rounds
and found we'd shot
two reasonable crocs
about 3 metres each.
With them lashed onto
the flat top ute back
totally illegal of course
we headed for home
but a cop stopped us
a block away
so we gave him some cheek
being 10 feet tall,
and bulletproof by now.
He arrested us all,
threw us in the pokey.
Nine months later
we went to court
were fined $4,500 each
and the bastard never returned

the evidence.

24

food for thought

Printed in Great Britain
by Amazon

73250530R00019